T0194191

THE
Glory
OF HIS
Presence

Pursuing the Presence that
Makes the Difference

GIDEON AKINSUYI

authorHOUSE®

AuthorHouse™
1663 Liberty Drive
Bloomington, IN 47403
www.authorhouse.com
Phone: 1 (800) 839-8640

Published by AuthorHouse 02/06/2020

ISBN: 978-1-7283-4594-9 (sc)
ISBN: 978-1-7283-4593-2 (e)

Library of Congress Control Number: 2020902338

Print information available on the last page.

"*And the Lord said unto Moses, I will do this thing also that thou hast spoken: for thou hast found grace in my sight, and I know thee by name. And he said, I beseech thee, shew me thy glory. And he said, I will make all my goodness pass before thee, and I will proclaim the name of the Lord before thee; and will be gracious to whom I will be gracious, and will shew mercy on whom I will shew mercy. And he said, Thou canst not see my face: for there shall no man see me, and live. And the Lord said, Behold, there is a place by me, and thou shalt stand upon a rock: And it shall come to pass, while my glory passeth by, that I will put thee in a clift of the rock, and will cover thee with my hand while I pass by: And I will take away mine hand, and thou shalt see my back parts: but my face shall not be seen.*" *Exodus 33:17-23*

Contents

Dedication

This book is dedicated to God the Father, Jesus the Son and the Holy Spirit my Comforter and greatest source of inspiration.

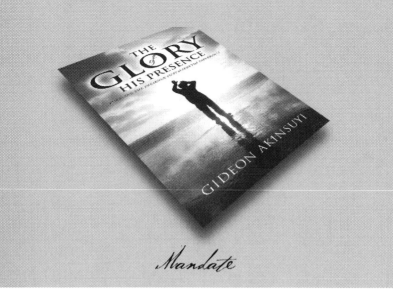

Mandate

Hate unrighteousness with passion and love righteousness with passion. Preach it hard and shout it everywhere for Christ is your example.

Acknowledgements

I am greatly indebted to all those who have contributed in one way or another to make this book a reality.

Daddy J.O Obayemi, the National Overseer RCCG. Out of your very busy schedules you created out the time to attend to me and accepted to write the foreword of this book. I am most grateful sir.

Daddy Julius Olalekan, the pastor in charge of Region, RCCG Region 12. Thank for your fatherly counsel and guidance. You made me see possibilities. Thank you very much sir.

Pastor Charles Awoyele thank you sir for taking time to read through the book and writing the introduction. Your professional touch and contributions are invaluable. You are highly appreciated sir.

Elder Kayode Matthew, thank you very much for proof reading this book and making the necessary corrections.

Introduction

The book titled THE GLORY OF HIS PRESENCE written by Pastor Gideon Akinsuyi is a symbolic 12 chapter book signaling the 12 tribes of Israel and seriously pontificating the goodness, likeness and presence of God as well as the necessity of the said glory in the lives of mankind. Meanwhile, I count it a huge privilege to be nominated by my amiable Pastor, astute/prolific writer and scholar to write the introduction of this un-put-down able *compendium with its lacing effect of wetting the appetites of heaven bound children of God as to the essentials of the Glory of His Presence. I will not take the privilege for granted and at the same time will not succumb to outburst sentiment at the expense meritorious appraisal of the merit of the book.*

The glory of God is so important in man's life that the absence of it spells doom on human existence. The writer of this book did not leave any stone unturned by putting the totality of the concept of the Glory of God in perspectives. The book is handy, style is mnemonic, language is simple and research is in-depth. It exposes all hidden treasures associated with glory before, now and to come which ought to engage the preoccupations of all preachers and scholars alike. Whosoever has experienced shame or embarrassment before being the opposite of glory, will find this book as a ready tool for quick restoration.

Christians are supposed to radiate the glory of God but many keep crawling under pity, sympathy, empathy and piteous lack of vision respectively thereby losing sight of the access to the glory made available by the cross. Why are Christians not experiencing shining in their different endeavors? Why do they run helter-skelter in pursuit of what is not lost? Amos 8; 12. These questions and many more find requisite response from the book.

When God appears in His glory, difficult circumstances will surely get His attention and time of sitting down in a pile of ashes to mourn sorrowful situations will yield automatically to BEAUTY. His glory creates appetite on people to want to be underneath the umbrella of His protection; His eyes upon us; His ears tuned to our cry. No wonder we are urged to live in the secret place of the most high and abide under His feathers and His wings for safety. The glory is put into hierarchical perspectives like glory of the sun, moon and stars; strolling glory, running and soaring glory altogether. When Peter saw a kind of glory on the mount of transfiguration, he hastily thought he saw it all, by concluding to end his journey there vide his suggestion of building three tents there one for

Moses, Elias and Jesus alike. The same Peter later gained unusual boldness to stand to responsibility on the day of Pentecost winning several souls with one message having seen greater glory. Glory then does not yield itself to any precise meaning but according to grace in attendance. As a corollary to all the suggested definitions of the author, one will see glory as the light that illuminates the darkness of the whole world but sometimes the light is so bright that one hardly sees anything again. In other words, the more you look the less you see. His glory is unsearchable sometimes, hence we see what He wants us to see.

Besides, it is customary of people in the bible time to mourn at every difficult time and lay in ashes. Is there anything beautiful about ashes? By His glory, we know God has promised to take your difficult, disgusting, depressing and horrible situations and give you beauty instead. He is going to pick you up out of ash pile of life and make something beautiful of you; moving you from your sugar kingdom to honey kingdom. Sometimes things that appear ugly just need the right climate to grow but we may not know unless by His mercy. I Samuel 30;6.

The glory of God is an enhancer of transformation and acceleration. This book is reminiscent of His promises to move us far and fast in life. John 6 ; 21.

Hannah was in tears and depressed- 1 Samuel 1;7 but when she encountered His glory, she laughed. Hezekiah was sick and near death- Isaiah 38; 3-5 but had 15 years elongation to his life on the platform of glory. His glory will cause flagrant departure from your past so that your future does not depend anymore on your past. Moses was nobody when his mother put him in a basket in the river. He had no identity but he was the one God has chosen to lead the children of Israel. He saw evil in his days but he did not stop there. Psalm 90; 15-16. He later saw the glory of God and he was speaking mouth to mouth with God in His glory. Those who saw Moses as ordinary later saw him in his glory and could not look straight into his eyes anymore.

Careful perusal of this book will bring us into an encounter with the Rhema behind Isaiah 60;20 which says ...your days of mourning shall be ended. Nobody who sees the glory of God is permitted to slide into mourning or error again.

A book like this is rare but a must read by all and sundry being an eye opener unto the workings of the glory of His presence which is an amalgam of His total presence in dominion giving hope to the hopeless by giving financial dominion to the poor. Eccle 9;16 says the voice of the poor will not be heard but when His glory comes, it will give the poor a voice and make him relevant for all purposes. No wonder Daniel was relevant back to back for three dispensations unhindered under the atmosphere of the glory of His presence. Daniel 6;27-28.

Money answers all things and money stops nonsense when glory chases away poverty. 2 corinthian 8;9.

Besides, there is glory in physical dominion also. Prov. 20;29. Little wonder Caleb said, my strength is as it was 45 years ago. No glory in disease and sickness. Hence, when you carry His glory, barrenness departs, curses depart and mountains melt down.

This book is a carrier of God's glory and anyone who reads or pretends to read it is also a carrier of His glory in overflow. There is a mandate of encounter associated with the reading and touching of this glorious book which gives due sense of responsibility. Acts 1;8 By virtue of the foregoing, it becomes imperative that responsibility without ability amounts to liability. This is the case of Moses who was not a slave but called upon to lead the slaves under the ambience that a slave cannot lead another slave. It takes a man with mandate to lead to compel obedience in motion on the part of others. Hence, mandate without mantle amounts to madness or a situation of searching for a virgin at the maternity home.

The most asked question as to how best can one appropriate the glory of God to one's life is favorably acceded to at the tail end of this book by signaling to the power of prayer and fasting. It then goes without saying that prayer is the price you pay to attain glory. Isaiah 58;6-8. The glory will be the resultant effect, so buy into that glory among other things with fasting. That is where many sold off their birthright. Luke 4;14

I therefore recommend this book for personal edification, development and refreshment for pastors, evangelists, teachers, students, ambitious educationists and those who may care to wonder the mystery of His glory. I make bold to recommend the book to all and sundry as a *PENDITA CUT OMEN {A BOOK TOO RELEVANT TO BE IGNORED}*

PASTOR CHARLES O.E. AWOYELE
LEGAL OFFICER RCCG YOUTH PROVINCE 2
PASTOR IN CHARGE OF AREA FULFILMENT AREA
YOUTH PROVINCE 2
LAGOS

Chapter One

THE GOD WE SERVE

"Give unto the Lord, O ye mighty, give unto the Lord glory and strength. Give unto the Lord the glory due unto his name; worship the Lord in the beauty of holiness. The voice of the Lord is upon the waters: the God of glory thundereth: the Lord is upon many waters." Psalm 29:1-3

The God we serve is the God of Glory. We are commanded to give Him the glory that is due to His name. How? By worshipping Him in the beauty of holiness. Associated with His glory is His holiness. God's glory and His holiness are inseparable. He is glorious in holiness.

Who is like unto thee, O Lord, among the gods? who is like thee, glorious in holiness, fearful in praises, doing wonders? Exodus 15:11

Associated also with His glory is His voice. When God speaks, His voice expresses His glory.

The voice of the Lord is upon the waters: the God of glory thundereth: the Lord is upon many waters. [4] The voice of the Lord is powerful; the voice of the Lord is full of majesty. Psalm 29:3-4

When you hear His voice regularly, you are gaining access to His glory.

The God we serve is not only the God of Glory, the Psalmist also calls Him the King of Glory.

Lift up your heads, O ye gates; and be ye lift up, ye everlasting doors; and the King of glory shall come in. [8] Who is this King of glory? The Lord strong and mighty, the Lord mighty in battle. [9] Lift up your heads, O ye gates; even lift them up, ye everlasting doors; and the King of glory shall come in. [10] Who is this King of glory? The Lord of hosts, he is the King of glory. Selah. Psalm 24:7-10

In those four verses of the scripture we are told that our God is the King. He has a kingdom and the nature of the kingdom is glory. This same truth is also established in Matthew. 6:13...*For thine is the kingdom, and the power, and the glory, for ever. Amen.*

The Psalmist went further to tell us who this King of Glory is; He is the Lord strong and mighty. The Lord mighty in battle, the Lord of hosts. So, associated with His Glory is His strength, might and ability.

In the book of Ephesians, Paul the apostle calls Him the father of Glory.

"That the God of our Lord Jesus Christ, the Father of glory, may give unto you the spirit of wisdom and revelation in the knowledge of him:" Ephesians **1:17**

So, associated with His glory is the spirit of wisdom, revelation and knowledge. He is the Father and source of glory.

In the book of Hebrews we are told that the Lord Jesus was crowned with glory and honour. He emptied himself of that glory and came down to die for humanity so that many of us can be restored to glory.

But we see Jesus, who was made a little lower than the angels for the suffering of death, crowned with glory and honour; that he by the grace of God should taste death for every man. [10] For it became him, for whom are all things, and by whom are all things, in bringing many sons unto glory, to make the captain of their salvation perfect through sufferings. Hebrews 2:9-10

In his letter to Timothy, Paul the apostle told him that the Lord Jesus is currently dwelling in a glorious light that no man can see with the natural eyes or approach unto.

Who only hath immortality, dwelling in the light which no man can approach unto; whom no man hath seen, nor can see: to whom be honour and power everlasting. Amen. 1 Timothy 6:16

The Psalmist also said the creation and all the works of God are speaking forth the glory of God. So, God created the universe as a means of expressing his glory.

The heavens declare the glory of God; and the firmament sheweth his handywork. Psalm 19:1

God's glory is very important to Him because it represents all that God is. So, God jealously guards and protects His glory. "*I am the Lord: that is my name: and my glory will I not give to another, neither my praise to graven images.*" *Isaiah. 42:8.*

All those who took his glory for granted in the wilderness were completely destroyed. They did not get to the promise land.

But as truly as I live, all the earth shall be filled with the glory of the LORD. Because all those men which have seen my glory, and my miracles, which I did in Egypt and in the wilderness, and have tempted me now these ten times, and have not hearkened to my voice; surely they shall not see the land which I sware unto their fathers, neither shall any of them that provoked me see it." Numbers. 14:21-23.

Chapter Two

CREATED FOR HIS GLORY

Even every one that is called by my name: for I have created him for my glory, I have formed him; yea, I have made him. Isaiah 43:7

You are created for God's glory. Don't let the devil lie to you at all, you are destined for a glorious life here on earth. It is your heritage as a child of God.

The very reason you were created is to exhibit the glory of God. The Psalmist caught a revelation of this and it was too much for him to comprehend.

What is man, that thou art mindful of him? and the son of man, that thou visitest him? For thou hast made him a little lower than the angels, and hast crowned him with glory and honour. Thou madest him to have dominion over the works of thy hands; thou hast put all things under his feet: Psalm 8:4-6

The devil doesn't want anyone to grasp this eternal truth and experience it. His utmost aim is to rob man of the glory of God and he does that by introducing sin into the lives of men.

The devil had enjoyed the glory of God's presence before but he lost it when iniquity was found in him. So, he does not want anyone else to enjoy what he has lost through rebellion.

Thou art the anointed cherub that covereth; and I have set thee so; thou wast upon the holy mountain of God; thou hast walked up and down in the midst of the stones of fire. Thou wast perfect in thy ways from the day that thou wast created, till iniquity was found in thee. Ezekiel 28:14-15

You are created for the glory of God and not for shame and ignominy. You were crowned with glory and honour at the very beginning. *Ps. 8:5.*

Everytime you have a doubt about the kind of life God intends for you to live here on earth, look back to the Garden of Eden and see the glorious life in the garden of God. That is God's plan for you; don't ever settle for less.

Adam and Eve were practically living in the glory of God, God came down to fellowship with them everyday. They saw his glory. They experienced the glory and carried it around here on earth.

The glory of God put Adam in charge here on earth. Every creature answered to him including all the dangerous and wild animals around. He was crowned with glory and honour. He was king of the earth reigning and ruling in glory.

When Adam sinned against God, what he lost was the glory of God. When he lost the glory he also lost every other thing. To God be the glory for allowing His Son to die a shameful death on the cross so that we might be restored back to glory.

But we see Jesus, who was made a little lower than the angels for the suffering of death, crowned with glory and honour; that he by the grace of God should taste death for every man. For it became him, for whom are all things, and by whom are all things, in bringing many sons unto glory, to make the captain of their salvation perfect through sufferings. Hebrews 2:9-10

Jesus came to defeat the devil, destroy his work and restore the lost glory.

He that committeth sin is of the devil; for the devil sinneth from the beginning. For this purpose the Son of God was manifested, that he might destroy the works of the devil. 1John 3:8

What the devil stole Jesus restored more abundantly. *The thief cometh not, but for to steal, and to kill, and to destroy: I am come that they might have life, and that they might have it more abundantly. John 10:10*

You are created for the glory of God and you must live a glorious life here on earth.

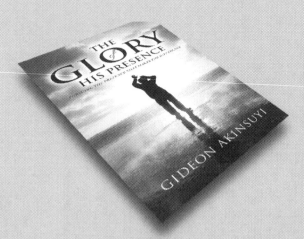

Chapter Three

SHOW ME YOUR GLORY

And he said, I beseech thee, shew me thy glory. Exodus 33:18

There is a point a man will get to in life and all the material blessings of life will no longer satisfy him.

This was exactly the experience of Moses at a point in his life. Moses and all Israel had experienced the deliverance of God. They had seen great miracles. God had provided for them. They had been protected from their enemies. God had always answered their prayers every time they prayed. God had promised an angel to lead them on in the journey and also protect them.

Yet Moses got to this point in his life where he was no longer satisfied with all that God had given but wanted God Himself. He cried out; ***show me thy glory. It is you I want now not just your angel, your provision, protection, promotion etc.***

Every one of us must get to this point in our lives because this is what it takes to make eternal impacts on earth. Life is much more than just receiving the blessings of God for yourself. As you walk on with the Lord you will get to this critical point where you will begin to ask yourself; "after the blessing and the promotion what next?"

You can get all the blessing you want; you will never find real fulfillment until God gives you Himself. Until He reveals His glory to you there will still be this hidden hunger within you that nothing else in this world can satisfy.

David got to this point in his life. He had been blessed, anointed, honoured and promoted by God, yet there was still this hunger for something beyond all of these in his heart.

O God, thou art my God; early will I seek thee: my soul thirsteth for thee, my flesh longeth for thee in a dry and thirsty land, where no water is; To see thy power and thy glory, so as I have seen thee in the sanctuary. Psalm 63:1-2

As the hart panteth after the water brooks, so panteth my soul after thee, O God. My soul thirsteth for God, for the living God: when shall I come and appear before God? Psalm 42:1-2

The apostle Paul also got to this point in his walk with God. He had seen special miracles and the blessings of God, yet there was a hunger in his heart beyond all of these.

That I may know him, and the power of his resurrection, and the fellowship of his sufferings, being made conformable unto his death; Philippians 3:10

God cannot be seen but His glory can be seen. It is in His manifest glory that He makes Himself known to those who are hungry for Him. It is when we get to this point of the knowledge of God based on the revelation of His glory that God becomes practically real to us and His strength and ability is imparted to us for great exploits in our world.

…but the people that do know their God shall be strong, and do exploits. Daniel 11:32

Moses was hungry for the manifest presence of God. He wanted to see the glory of God and he saw it because he was desperate enough for it. He saw it and his life was never the same again. He contacted the glory he saw and became a carrier of the same. He ended up becoming a wonder to his generation. No man can see the glory of God and ever remain the same again.

God is looking for hungry and desperate people who want to see His glory at any cost. People who are ready to pray-through to the revelation of the glory and become an instrument in the hand of God to shine forth the light of His glory in their generation.

Are you available?

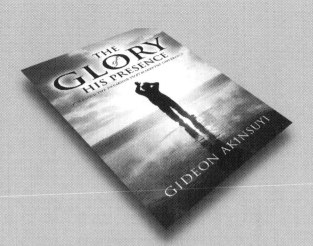

Chapter Four

GLORY DEFINED

And he said, I beseech thee, shew me thy glory. And he said, I will make all my goodness pass before thee, and I will proclaim the name of the Lord before thee; and will be gracious to whom I will be gracious, and will shew mercy on whom I will shew mercy. Exodus 33:18-19

Glory has been described as magnificence, great beauty, brightness, splendor, brilliance or glamour.

Scripturally, glory is one of those words that are difficult to define. There seems to be not just one straight meaning for it. There is just not one definition sufficient for it. For example, according to Proverbs Glory is the opposite of shame. *"the wise shall inherit glory; but shame shall be the promotion of fools" Proverbs. 3:25.*

Since the opposite of the wise is the fools then, we can safely conclude that what the wise will inherit, which is glory: is the opposite of shame which the fools will inherit.

In essence, this verse of the scripture is saying, when you are wise in the sight of God, walking in His ways and principles you will ultimately access and enjoy the glory of God. However, if you are a fool not walking in the ways of God but living in disobedience to His principles and commandments, then you will end your journey in shame.

So, what is the glory of God? From the text we saw Moses cried to the Lord, *"show me thy glory"* and the Lord answered in response to his request. *"I will make <u>all my goodness</u> pass before thee, and I will proclaim the name of the Lord before thee, and will be gracious to whom I will be gracious".*

From these verses of the scripture we can say the glory of God is the manifestation of God in all of his goodness, brightness, majesty, power, holiness, excellence etc. revealed to a man. Not some or most of His goodness but all of His goodness. This was what Moses saw; the manifestation of all His goodness.

When you put all of the goodness of God together, it will produce only one thing and that thing is called glory. So, you see that the glory of God is not just one thing but a product of all the goodness of God put together.

This is very interesting. When I was in secondary school I did a little of physics and we were taught Dispersion of

Light. I found something very interesting here that can be related to this. When white light is passed through a triangular prism, the white light is separated into its component colours; red, orange, yellow green, blue and violet. So, what we call a white light is actually a combination of almost all the colours of the rainbow, one beautiful light.

The glory of God is something similar to this. It is not just one thing but a combination of all the goodness of God revealed to a man. God is everywhere but he does not manifest everywhere. It is only where He manifests Himself that His glory is revealed.

Chapter Five

THE GLIMPSE OF HIS GLORY

And the Lord descended in the cloud, and stood with him there, and proclaimed the name of the Lord. And the Lord passed by before him, and proclaimed, The Lord, The Lord God, merciful and gracious, longsuffering, and abundant in goodness and truth, Exodus 34:5-6

The Lord God answered the prayer of Moses. He cried to see the glory of God and the Lord decided to come down and introduce himself and make his glory known to Moses.

As we can see in this passage when the Lord came down in the fullness of his glory, the first thing he did was to introduce himself to Moses so that Moses could have an accurate knowledge of God. Moses has been taught of the Lord by his parents before this time yet he has not known the Lord as he ought to. He has been called of God and has been walking with God and working for God yet he has not known the Lord as he ought to.

However, when God heard his cry for the revelation of His glory and came down to show him his glory, Moses came to the place of practical knowledge of God beyond what he has been taught. It is the revelation of the glory of God to a man that brings the practical and experiential knowledge of God. Until God reveals himself he can't really be known.

Secondly, the revelation of God in the fullness of his glory brought Moses to his knees in worship. *"And Moses made haste, and bowed his head toward the earth and worshipped". Exodus 34:8.*

Prior to this time, Moses had been speaking with God, yet it was not recorded at any point in time that he bowed down and worshipped. However, on this occasion, something was different. He made haste, bowed down and worshipped, what has changed? Moses saw himself as he was for the first time in the light of God's glory and became humbled. It is in the revelation of the glory of God to us that we get to see ourselves as we are and become humble in his sight.

This was exactly what happened to Isaiah the prophet in Isaiah 6:1-5. After he caught a revelation of God in the fullness of his glory, he saw himself and became humble. *"Then said I, woe is me for I am undone, because I am a man of unclean lips and I dwell in the midst of a people of unclean lips; for my eyes have seen the king, the Lord of host" Isaiah 6:5.*

When a man sees the revelation of God in the fullness of His glory, he naturally comes down from his high horse and become humble before God. At the sight of His glorious majesty, pride naturally dies. When you see the glory of God, the true worship of God becomes natural for you.

The third thing that happened to Moses after he saw the Lord in the fullness of his glory was that he was able to see the people of God differently and became moved with compassion towards them. *"And he said, if now I have found grace in thy sight O Lord let my Lord I pray thee go among us, for it is a stiff-necked people and pardon our iniquity and our sin and take us for thine inheritance"* Exo. 34:9.

There is something about the glory of God revealed to a man that births compassion for people in him. When you see God in the fullness of his glory and you see yourself the way you are and become humbled by the glory of His presence; then you begin to see the people created in His image differently and become moved with compassion towards them.

This also happened to prophet Isaiah after he saw the glory of God. He saw himself and became humbled before the Lord. He saw his unworthiness, uncleanliness, unrighteousness and unqualified state and humbled himself. The angel of the Lord took a live coal from the altar and put it upon his tongue to purify and purge away his sin and iniquity.

Then flew one of the seraphims unto me, having a live coal in his hand, which he had taken with the tongs from off the altar: And he laid it upon my mouth, and said, Lo, this hath touched thy lips; and thine iniquity is taken away, and thy sin purged. Isaiah 6:6-7

After all the personal revelation and personal transformation by the glory of God, his heart went out in compassion towards his people. *"Also I heard the voice of the Lord; saying whom shall I send and who will go for us" then said I, here am I, send me", Isaiah 6:8.*

The revelation of God's glory brings personal transformation. It changes a man from inside out. It affects the way a man sees God, himself and other people. The glory of His presence changes a man spirit, soul and body.

You cannot catch a glimpse of His glory and remain the same in your attitude towards God or towards God people. God cannot reveal His glory to you and pride will still have a hold on your life; impossible. You will come down from your high horse, you will be completely transformed.

The radical transformation of Saul, the persecutor to Paul, the apostle of the gentiles was as a result of his encounter with the Glory of God on the road to Damascus. The appearance of the Lord Jesus to him in the fullness of his glory brought him down from his high horse and changed him completely from inside out.

And as he journeyed, he came near Damascus: and suddenly there shined round about him a light from heaven: And he fell to the earth, and heard a voice saying unto him, Saul,

Saul, why persecutest thou me? And he said, Who art thou, Lord? And the Lord said, I am Jesus whom thou persecutest: it is hard for thee to kick against the pricks. And he trembling and astonished said, Lord, what wilt thou have me to do? And the Lord said unto him, Arise, and go into the city, and it shall be told thee what thou must do. Acts 9:3-6

Every encounter with God's glory brings transformation. You can never encounter and experience the glory of God and remain the same.

Chapter Six

CARRIERS OF HIS GLORY

And he was there with the Lord forty days and forty nights; he did neither eat bread, nor drink water. And he wrote upon the tables the words of the covenant, the ten commandments. And it came to pass, when Moses came down from mount Sinai with the two tables of testimony in Moses' hand, when he came down from the mount, that Moses wist not that the skin of his face shone while he talked with him. And when Aaron and all the children of Israel saw Moses, behold, the skin of his face shone; and they were afraid to come nigh him. Exodus 34:28-30

God wants all of us His children to be carriers of His glory. He told us in Isaiah 43:7 that this is what we are created for. *"Even everyone that is called by my name; for I have created him for my glory, I have formed him; ye I have made him".*

We thank God that this is possible because Moses did not just see the glory of God, he became a carrier of His glory. Moses was with God on the mountain for 40 days and 40 nights communing and fellowshipping with God. For those 40 days and 40 nights, he did not eat or drink. It was in those 40 days that he learnt the ways of God and wrote the words of the covenant between God and Israel on the fables. There he wrote the Ten Commandments with his hands.

When Moses came down from the mountain after 40 days and 40 nights of dwelling in the glory of God; Aaron and all the people that saw him were afraid of him. They began to run away from him because of the brightness of the glory shining on his face. Moses became a carrier of His glory because he had seen the glory and stayed long enough in the glory.

From that point on, Moses had to put a veil on his face before he could face the children of Israel to talk with them because of the brightness of the light of God's glory shinning on his face. He literally became a god to the children of Israel, an oracle they had to consult in order to experience the acts of God. ***"He made known his ways unto Moses, his acts unto the children of Israel. Psalm 103:7***

When God reveals his glory to a man, he reveals his glory in him also. When a man looks at God long enough, he begins to look like God. When a man dwells long enough in the glory of God he becomes a carrier of His glory.

The glory is available for those who are willing to pay the price. Moses paid the price and carried the glory with which he affected his generation for God. He was desperate in prayers *Exo. 33:18*. He waited on the Lord for 40 days and 40 nights. He sacrificed in fasting; completely denied himself of food and water.

People who carried the glory of God in their generation were people who were desperate for the glory. They hungered for the glory above every other thing. They sacrificed greatly. They paid the price.

David was desperate for the glory of God and he carried it to affect his generation for God. He was desperate in prayers. ***"O God thou art my God; early will I seek thee. My soul thirsteth for thee, my flesh longeth for thee in a dry and thirsty land where no water is. To see thy power and thy glory, so as I have seen thee in the sanctuary"*** *Psalm. 63:1-3.*

People who will carry the glory of God also in this generation must be people who are ready to wait on the Lord until the glory rest on them. The glory of God is not for those who cannot wait in His presence. It is for those who can spend quality time with him. They must be ready to sacrifice in fasting and prayer until the glory comes.

There is a price to pay to carry the glory of God for your generation. Even the Lord Jesus who carried the glory of the only begotten Son of the Father paid the price for the glory he carried to affect his generation. Scriptures told us that he waited on the Lord for 40 days and 40 nights before the glory that made the difference came upon

Him. He would have lived as a carpenter for the rest of His life without the glory, *Lk. 4:1-14*.

Those who carry His glory naturally make a difference in their world. When they show up where darkness is reigning, they take charge while darkness naturally gives way to them. What the glory does is to announce you to your world as you become a solution to their problems.

Chapter Seven

AFFECTED BY THE GLORY

He made known his ways unto Moses, his acts unto the children of Israel. Psalm 103:7

When God shows you His glory you become a carrier of His glory and then you become affected by the glory you carry. When the glory rests upon a man his life does not remain the same again.

Moses saw the glory of God, became a carrier of the glory and his entire life was affected by that glory. The glory of God affected his spirit, soul and body.

The encounter Moses had with the glory of God so quickened his spirit that he could operate at the frequency of God. Moses could understand all spiritual things and mysteries. His spirit was so invaded by the glory of God that he was able to gain access into the realm of the spirit and uncover for us what happened at creation even though he was not physically there when the world began.

Nothing quickens the human spirit like the glory of God invading it. It brings a man to the place of supernatural understanding. *"There is a spirit in man and the inspiration of the Almighty giveth them understanding." Job 32:8.*

How was Moses able to know what happened in the beginning? He saw the back part of God and caught a glimpse of the glory of God. Not only that; he also saw the events of the past because they are all hidden in God.

"And the Lord said, behold there is a place by me and thou shall stand upon a rock and it shall come to pass while my glory passeth by that I will put thee in a chift of the rock, and will cover thee with my hand while I pass by; And I will take away mine hand and thou shall see my back parts; but my face shall not be seen." Exo. 33:21-23.

The glory also affected the soul of Moses. His mind and thinking faculty was also invaded by the glory of God. *"He made know his ways unto Moses, his acts unto the children of Israel." Psalm 103:7.*

God made known His ways unto Moses by revealing His glory to him. All secrets and mysteries are hidden in God; so, the revelation of the glory and presence of God to a man is equally an access into the mysteries that are hidden in him.

His ways are not our ways but His ways are higher and better than our ways.

THE GLORY OF HIS PRESENCE

"My thoughts are not your thoughts neither are your ways my ways saith the LORD. For as the heavens are higher than the earth, so are my ways higher than your ways and my thoughts higher than your thoughts" Isaiah 55:9.

The influence of the glory of God on the soul of Moses enabled him to think the thoughts of God. The glory of His presence enables a man to appreciate His ways above human ways. It will enable us to drop own our ways to follow His own ways.

The glory of God's presence also affected the body of Moses. He enjoyed supernatural health here on earth. It was not recorded once in the Bible that Moses was sick. At a point in his life he was doing alone the work of seventy people and he was still very normal and fit. He didn't feel it at all health wise.

His entire body was so invaded by the glory he carried that there was no room for sickness to stay there. Till the day of his death, the glory of God was rejuvenating his entire system.

"And Moses was an hundred and twenty years old when he died. His eyes was not dim nor his natural force abated." Deut. 34:7.

Nothing renews a man's life like the glory of God. People who stay in the presence of God to experience and carry His glory don't fall sick like others. The glory renews their cells, tissues, organs and entire system regularly.

The reason why angels don't fall sick or grow old is because of the glory of God they are constantly exposed to. There is no room for corruption or decay where the glory of God dwells. The reason why we will not die again in eternity is because the glory of God will be our light forever there. There will be no need for the sun or moon there. The one who sits upon the throne will be our light.

The sun shall be no more thy light by day; neither for brightness shall the moon give light unto thee: but the Lord shall be unto thee an everlasting light, and thy God thy glory. Isaiah 60:19

And there shall be no night there; and they need no candle, neither light of the sun; for the Lord God giveth them light: and they shall reign for ever and ever. Revelation 22:5

THE GLORY OF HIS PRESENCE

GIDEON AKINSUYI

Chapter Eight

WHERE THE GLORY DWELLS

And the ark of the Lord continued in the house of Obed-edom the Gittite three months: and the Lord blessed Obed-edom, and alls his household. And it was told king David, saying, The Lord hath blessed the house of Obed-edom, and all that pertaineth unto him, because of the ark of God. So David went and brought up the ark of God from the house of Obed-edom into the city of David with gladness. 2 Samuel 6:11-12

Where the glory of God dwells, unusual things happen. In the scripture above we saw how the glory of God's presence in the house of Obededom brought strange blessings to him. The glory of God practically transformed and turned around his life within the space of three months.

The truth is that God is present everywhere; that's why He is called the Omnipresent. However, He does not just manifest Himself everywhere. It is only where he chooses to manifest Himself that the glory of His presence is being revealed. That is where His power, miracles, blessings and all His goodness will be released.

The ark of God that represented the presence of God stayed in the house of this man for only three months and he became an envy of the entire nation. Even king David envied him. The glory so manifested that everything about Obededom became strangely blessed. Where the glory dwells curses are cancelled and replaced with blessings. The kind of blessings that make rich and a whole nation will begin to talk about it.

So, where the glory dwells that is where wealth and riches also dwell. Where the glory dwells all needs are met. Paul was praying for the Philippians church after they ministered to his needs that his God will supply all their needs out of the riches of his glory.

But my God shall supply all your need according to his riches in glory by Christ Jesus. Philippians 4:19

There are unsearchable riches and wealth inside the glory of God and where the glory dwells they become manifest.

"The silver is mine and the gold is mine saith the Lord of hosts. The glory of this latter house shall be greater than of the former saith the Lord of hosts…" Haggai 2:8-9.

The glory of God cannot be separated from the wealth of God; because what makes up the glory of God in the first place is all His goodness according to.

And he said, I will make all my goodness pass before thee, and I will proclaim the name of the Lord before thee; and will be gracious to whom I will be gracious, and will shew mercy on whom I will shew mercy. Exodus 33:19

As the glory dwelt in the house of Obededom for three months wealth and prosperity also dwelt there.

What made all the difference in the life of Obededom? The Glory of God. Not only was God present in his house, His Glory was revealed there. Remember that God can be present in a place and not manifests Himself there. It is only where He manifests Himself that we see His power and glory at work.

Notice that the same ark that represents the very presence of God was in the house of a man called Abinadab before it was brought to the house of Obededom. The ark was there for about 40 years yet this man was not blessed like Obededom. What made the difference between these two men? I will discuss that extensively in Chapter 10. Just remember that God can be present in a place and not reveal Himself or manifest His glory there.

Where the glory of God dwells there is preservation and protection from all attacks of the enemy. The glory becomes an hedge surrounding the carrier making him unreachable for the enemy. This is what the devil said concerning Job.

"Then Satan answered the LORD and saith. Doth Job fear God for nought? Hast not thou made an hedge about him and about his house and about all that he hath on every side? Thou has blessed the work of his hands and his substance is increased in the land". Job. 1:9-10.

There was an hedge of glory over and around Job and his household. That led to the blessing of all the works of his hand and the increase of all his substances just like that of Obededom. Then that became a protection for him against the attack of the devil. Until God took away the hedge of his glory from Job and his family, the devil couldn't attack him.

It was the same cloud of Glory that protected the children of Israel in the wilderness. They needed not to be afraid of any attack while God was leading them by the cloud of His glory. When they sinned and God told them He was not going to lead them on any longer and made arrangement for an angel to continue leading them; Moses cried out, if your presence does not go with me, carry us not up from here.

And he said unto him, If thy presence go not with me, carry us not up hence. For wherein shall it be known here that I and thy people have found grace in thy sight? is it not in that thou goest with us? so shall we be separated, I and thy people, from all the people that are upon the face of the earth. Exodus 33:15-16

The glory cloud made them the apples of God's eyes and untouchable for the enemy. ***He found him in a desert land, and in the waste howling wilderness; he led him about, he instructed him, he kept him as the apple of his eye.*** *Deuteronomy 32:10*

For thus saith the Lord of hosts; After the glory hath he sent me unto the nations which spoiled you: for he that toucheth you toucheth the apple of his eye. *Zechariah 2:8*

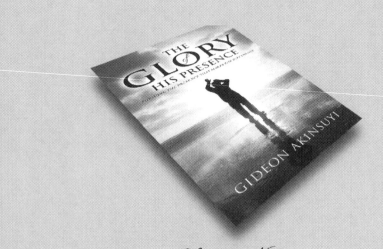

Chapter Nine

IN HIS PRESENCE

Thou wilt shew me the path of life: in thy presence is fulness of joy; at thy right hand there are pleasures for evermore. Psalm 16:11

Where the glory of His presence is manifested, there is no yoke of the devil or anything that causes sorrows can survive there. The glory of His presence destroys yokes and turns sorrows to joy.

In 2008 we wanted to have the one year anniversary of a monthly programme I was running in my parish then as a very young pastor. The programme was tagged Night of Destiny. It was always a night of serious warfare and deliverance. The Lord did some strange things in those meetings as we gathered every month.

As we were preparing for the one year anniversary of the programme; I had a leading that the LORD wanted us to have three nights consecutively as against the usual one night a month and make it purely night of worship and high praises alone with the theme; IN HIS PRESENCE.

The Lord also instructed that we should anoint everyone each night after each session of praises and worship for the three nights. We printed flyers and invited people all around for the programme to join us in praising the Lord.

On the first day of the programme as I was coming into the church before the programme began, I met a woman heavily pregnant with her husband by her both waiting to see me. She narrated her ordeal. "Sir I heard about this programme and that's why I am here but I need to explain some things to you first before the programme will start.

My problem is this pregnancy I am carrying, I have carried it for two years and four months already and the baby has refused to come down. I have gone to churches and mountains for deliverance sessions, but the baby has refused to come down. They told me that evil forces used to come and carry the baby out of my womb at night and bring it back.

I have prayed and done all that I know how to do yet the baby has refused to come down. I believe God will deliver me someday.

As a young pastor in my twenties I was very scared. I have been hearing stories like that before, they always sounded like fairy tales but now I am face to face with one. So, I tried not to give her any false hope at all. I said, "Madam I am very sorry but this is not a deliverance service ma.

The Lord just instructed us to praise and worship Him for three nights and that is what we are here to do. Then I added, if you will join us to praise Him anything can happen in His presence, she said I will sir.

So, I held her hand with her husband's hand and prayed a short prayer for them in my office before the programme began that night.

The first night was awesome. We sang praises in high spirits and danced to the Lord. All the young people were shouting and jumping in praises to God all through the night. Then I saw this woman in her own corner with her big belly shouting, dancing and praising God with the youth.

Every time I looked in her direction, I got scared, quickly said a prayer for her in my heart pleading with God not to let her fall down inside our church as she was really doing it; making effort to jump as if nothing was at stake. We finished the first night and everyone was anointed with oil before we closed the service.

The second night, this woman was back in our church for the programme, we had another great time in His presence. At the end of the second night everyone was anointed again and we departed.

On the third and final day of the programme this woman did not show up and I didn't even remember because she was not a member of my church, she had only come for the special programme. We had another wonderful time as the programme came to the peak that night as if we should not end it.

On Saturday that same weekend, I was resting in my house from the pressure of the programme and the sleepless nights; I got a call and it was from this woman. After she introduced herself I said, sister how are you? We didn't see you the last day of the programme. She said, yes sir, after the second night of praise and worship I began to feel serious labour pain so I went to the hospital. As I speak with you sir, I have a bouncing baby boy after two years and four months of pregnancy. I shouted praise the Lord.

Do you know what happened to this woman? She encountered the glory of God's presence activated by praise and worship and that destroyed the yoke in her life, turning her sorrow to joy.

In the course of our intense worship and praises to the Almighty God; the glory of His presence filled the church and her yoke was destroyed; whatever was tying her baby down was completely removed.

Where the glory of His presence dwell no yoke of the devil can survive. All works of the devil will be naturally destroyed. In His presence anything can happen.

Chapter Ten

REACTING OR RESPONDING?

And they set the ark of God upon a new cart, and brought it out of the house of Abinadab that was in Gibeah: and Uzzah and Ahio, the sons of Abinadab, drave the new cart. And they brought it out of the house of Abinadab which was at Gibeah, accompanying the ark of God: and Ahio went before the ark. 2 Samuel 6:3-4

This is one of the most instructive passages for me in the Bible. The Ark of God was present in the houses of two different individuals and the two of them had two different experiences with the same Ark.

One person was so blessed in a strange way within the three months the Ark dwelt in his house that he became the talk of the town. For about 40 years before, the same Ark was in the house of another man yet he was not blessed. Not only was he not blessed, the day the Ark of God was taken out of his house God killed his son.

THE GLORY OF HIS PRESENCE

The same Ark, representing the presence of the Almighty God. The same presence but different results. What happened? What made the difference between these two people? Why are they having different results in the presence of the same God? One was reacting to the presence while the other was responding.

This exactly explains the reason why God can be present in a place among a people and some will be experiencing His blessings; getting better and sharing testimonies every time, while others will be getting worse and complaining everyday.

What does it mean to react? It means to act in response to someone or something in a particular way that is rebellious and opposing. It simply means to retaliate. For whatever reason Abinadab was reacting to the presence of the Ark of God in his house for about 40 years and because of that God could not manifest Himself. Remember, God can be in a place and not manifest Himself there. It is only where He manifests Himself that His glory will be revealed bringing about the release of His blessings.

A critical look at the circumstances surrounding the Ark of God coming into the house of Abinadab will give us some clues as to why this priest who should know God better was reacting to Him instead of responsing to Him.

The story began in *1 Samuel Chapter 4.* Israel went to war against the Philistine in days of Eli the priest. Israel suffered defeat as they were smitten by the Philistines. About 4000 soldiers of Israel died and Israel fled before their enemies.

Then it occurred to the elders that the reason for their defeat was because God was not among them in the battle field; so, they decided to bring the Ark of God from Shiloh into the battle field. Now the two sons of Eli, Hophini and Phinehas were in charge of the Ark of God at that time. Unfortunately, their ways were not right in the sight of God.

*1 Samuel 2:12. **"Now the sons of Eli were sons of Belial, they knew not the Lord"***

They had so provoked God to anger that He vowed to judge their father and his entire household in His anger.

*1 Samuel 3:12-14 **"In that day I will perform against Eli all the things that I have spoken concerning his house when I begin I will also make an end. For I have told him that I will judge his house forever for the iniquity which he knoweth, because his sons made themselves vile and he restrained them not. And therefore I have sworn unto the house of Eli, that the iniquity of Eli house shall not be purged with sacrifice nor offering forever"***

Imagine! A people with whom the Lord had indignation; yet they were the ones carrying the Ark of God to the battle field. You can readily predict what will happen.

So the people sent to Shiloh, that they might bring from thence the ark of the covenant of the Lord of hosts, which dwelleth between the cherubims: and the two sons of Eli, Hophni and Phinehas, were there with the ark of the covenant of God. And when the ark of the covenant of the Lord came into the camp, all Israel shouted with a great shout, so that the earth rang again. And when the Philistines heard the noise of the shout, they said, What meaneth the noise of this great shout in the camp of the Hebrews? And they understood that the ark of the Lord was come into the camp. And the Philistines were afraid, for they said, God is come into the camp. And they said, Woe unto us! for there hath not been such a thing heretofore. Woe unto us! who shall deliver us out of the hand of these mighty Gods? these are the Gods that smote the Egyptians with all the plagues in the wilderness. Be strong, and quit yourselves like men, O ye Philistines, that ye be not servants unto the Hebrews, as they have been to you: quit yourselves like men, and fight. And the Philistines fought, and Israel was smitten, and they fled every man into his tent: and there was a very great slaughter; for there fell of Israel thirty thousand footmen. And the ark of God was taken; and the two sons of Eli, Hophni and Phinehas, were slain. And there ran a man of Benjamin out of the army, and came to Shiloh the same day with his clothes rent, and with earth upon his head. And when he came, lo, Eli sat upon a seat by the wayside watching: for his heart trembled for the ark of God. And when the man came into the city, and told it, all the city cried out. And when Eli heard the noise of the crying, he said, What meaneth the noise of this tumult? And the man came in hastily, and told Eli. Now Eli was ninety and eight years old; and his eyes were dim, that he could not see. And the man said unto Eli, I am he that came out of the army, and I fled to day out of the army. And he said, What is there done, my son? And the messenger answered and said, Israel is fled before the Philistines, and there hath been also a great slaughter among the people, and thy two sons also, Hophni and Phinehas, are dead, and the ark of God is taken. And it came to pass, when he made mention of the ark of God, that he fell from off the seat backward by the side of the gate, and his neck brake, and he died: for he was an old man, and heavy. And he had judged Israel forty years. 1 Samuel 4:4-18

Wherever sin and disobedience are reigning God does not manifest Himself. The glory of God can never be revealed to those who live in rebellion against Him. Even though He was present there He chooses not to manifest Himself. He chooses not to reveal His glory among them.

MANIFESTATION IN THE HOUSE OF DAGON

When you read 1 Samuel chapter 5 it will amaze you that the same God who decided not to manifest Himself in the battle field where there were many soldiers ready to fight for Him is now fighting for Himself without the aid of any soldier.

He attacked the god of the Philistines called Dagon and destroyed it. His hand was against all the priests of Dagon and all the people of the land. Every city they took the

Ark to from Ashdod to Gath to Ekron God's hand was heavy upon them and they were seriously dealt with.

It is very instructive to know that God can defend Himself, He can fight for Himself. It is therefore a great privilege and honour to be enlisted in the army of the Lord; and this honour must never be taken lightly.

We have the duty as children of God to live our lives in such a way that will allow our God who is present with us to always manifest Himself among us and show us His power and glory. Every time we live in disobedience and rebellion we miss the opportunity to see God manifest Himself to us and show us His glory.

THE JOURNEY TO THE HOUSE OF ABINADAB

The story continued in *1 Samuel Chapter 6*. The Ark of God was in the land of the Philistines for seven months. God dealt with them from city to city until they were told what to do in order to be free from the anger of God. They were advised to send the Ark of God back to Israel with a trespass offering and not harden their hearts like the Egyptians and Pharaoh.

They made a new cart and put all the jewels of gold for their trespass offering in it beside the Ark and tied it to a kine and sent it away. Amazingly by itself the animal took the Ark and the trespass offering back to the border of Israel in Beth-Shemesh where it was received and sacrifices were made unto God by the priest.

After that, the people began to look into the Ark and God was angry with them.

And he smote the men of Beth-shemesh, because they had looked into the ark of the Lord, even he smote of the people fifty thousand and threescore and ten men: and the people lamented, because the Lord had smitten many of the people with a great slaughter. And the men of Beth-shemesh said, Who is able to stand before this holy Lord God? and to whom shall he go up from us? And they sent messengers to the inhabitants of Kirjath-jearim, saying, The Philistines have brought again the ark of the Lord ; come ye down, and fetch it up to you. 1 Samuel 6:19-21

They took God for granted and they paid dearly for it. God is good but He is not a gentle man.

Finally they had to bring the Ark of God into the house of this priest called Abinadab.

"And the men of Kirjath Jearim came and fetched up the Ark of the Lord and brought it into the house of Abinadab in the hill, and sanctified Eleazar his son to keep the Ark of the Lord." 1samuel 7:1

That was how the Ark of the God of Israel got to the house of Abinadab. The very first personal house the Ark of God would dwell. The Ark got to his house before Saul became King and throughout the 40years of the reign of king Saul the Ark was in his house. So, the Ark was in his house for more than 40years. Saul was not interested in the Ark. It didn't mean much to him like it meant to David.

For all the years the ark was in the house of this priest called Abinadab God did not manifest Himself there, His glory was not revealed and this man was not blessed in any special way. The day the Ark was taken out of his house his son was careless with the Ark and God killed him.

Yet the same Ark was in the house of another man for three months and the difference was clear. God manifested Himself in the house of Obededom. His glory was revealed and strange blessings followed.

We know from scriptures that there is no respect of person with God. Act 10:34-35.**" Then Peter opened his mouth and said of a truth I perceive that God is no respecter of persons. But in every nation he that feareth him and worketh righteousness, is accepted with him."**

For over 40years Abinadab and his house were not responding to the presence of God in their house rather they were reacting; whether knowingly or unknowingly and that prevented God from manifesting Himself among them. Their attitude towards the Ark was not right.

I am sure the Ark was not treated with the kind of honour and reverence it deserved. What played out on the way that led to the death of Uzah is a clue to what has been happening behind closed doors in the house of Abinadab. God must have endured Abinadab and his children' attitudes toward the Ark all those years until that day when He could not endure them anymore.

Don't ever be too familiar with God. Never take Him for granted. He is a good God but not a gentle man. He is a consuming fire.

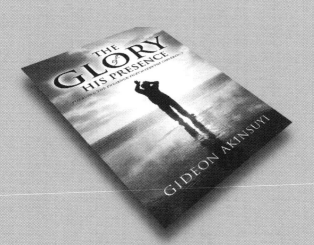

Chapter Eleven

ENFORCING THE GLORY

Give unto the Lord, O ye mighty, give unto the Lord glory and strength. Give unto the Lord the glory due unto his name; worship the Lord in the beauty of holiness. The voice of the Lord is upon the waters: the God of glory thundereth: the Lord is upon many waters. The voice of the Lord is powerful; the voice of the Lord is full of majesty. Psalm 29:1-4

Our God is referred to here as the God of Glory. This God who is present everywhere but does not manifest Himself everywhere can be made to begin to thunder where He had been hitherto quiet.

In order words there is something to do to make the God of Glory thunder and cause His voice to be heard where He had earlier hid Himself and remained silent. His voice that is powerful and full of majesty can be heard where He had not been heard. He can begin to manifest Himself and show forth His glory when we respond appropriately to His presence.

Looking at the passage above and other scripture we will see how to respond to His presence and activate his glory in a place.

GIVE UNTO THE LORD

The first thing the psalmist said here to activate the glory is *"Give Unto the Lord"* Ps 29:1

Giving sacrificially and generously to the Lord is one sure way to activate His glory in a place. Every time sacrificial offerings are accepted God manifested Himself and revealed His glory.

"Now when Solomon had made an end of praying, the fire came down from heaven and consumed the burnt offering and the sacrifices, and the priest could not enter into the house of the lord because the glory of the Lord had filled the Lord's house", 2 Chronicles 7:1-2.

When we give generously to God out of love and in response to His love for us we activate the manifestation of His glory where we are.

Solomon understood this very well. Since the very first time he offered unto God when he newly became king over Israel, he prepared an unusual offering and sacrifices to God and that made God to manifest Himself in His glory to Solomon that very night.

THE GLORY OF HIS PRESENCE

"And Solomon loved the Lord, walking in the statutes of David his father; only he sacrificed and burnt incense in high places. And the king went to Gibeon to sacrifice there; for that was the great high place: a thousand burnt offerings did Solomon offer upon that altar in Gibeon the Lord appeared to Solomon in a dream by night; and said ask what I shall give thee" 1 kings 3:3-5.

Since that first encounter Solomon had learnt to prepare an unusual sacrifice every time he wanted the manifestation of God and the revelation of his glory.

GIVE UNTO THE LORD GLORY AND HONOUR

We respond to God's presence in a place by giving Him glory and honour. We are commanded to give him the glory that is due to His name. Every time we fail to give glory to God and accord Him the honour that is due to Him we are not responding appropriately to his presence.

When we honour the Lord and approach Him with reverential awe; we are giving Him the glory that is due to His name. When we live in the consciousness of His Almightiness and approach Him with holy fear. Then we are preparing the ground for His manifestation and the revelation of his glory to us.

God does not manifest His glory where He is being dishonored or taken for granted. Instead of manifesting His glory; wherever He is being dishonored what people experience is His anger.

GIDEON AKINSUYI

WORSHIP THE LORD IN THE BEAUTY OF HOLINESS

Genuine worship and praises is another way of activating His glory in a place. We know that God inhabits the praises of His people. Ps 22:3. Every time His people praise Him in truth and in spirit they are responding to His presence and activating His glory among them.

"And it came to pass as the trumpeters and singers were as one to make one sound to be heard in praising and thanking the Lord and when they lifted up their voice with the trumpets and cymbals and instruments of music, and praised the Lord saying, for he is good; for his mercy endureth forever: that then the house was filled with cloud, even the house of the Lord. So, that the priests could not stand to minister by reason of the cloud, for the glory of the Lord had filled the House of God". 2chro 5:13-14.

Pure and unadulterated worship is one of the surest ways of activating the glory of God. Even among angels in heaven this is the model and pattern.

In the year that king Uzziah died I saw also the Lord sitting upon a throne, high and lifted up, and his train filled the temple. Above it stood the seraphims: each one had six wings; with twain he covered his face, and with twain he covered his feet, and with twain he did fly. And one cried unto another, and said, Holy, holy, holy, is the Lord of hosts: the whole earth is full of his glory. And the posts of the door moved at the voice of him that cried, and the house was filled with smoke. Isaiah 6:1-4

The angels are constantly exposed to the glory of His presence and the impact of that is very enormous on them. They don't grow old or get sick because the glory of His presence keeps them continuously renewed; However, they have to continue to worship Him in the beauty of holiness to continue to enjoy the glory of His presence.

SPIRITUAL ROMANCE

Another way of responding to the presence and activating His glory is by loving Him and showing it with obedient action.

"He that hath my commandments, and keepeth them, he it is that loveth me: and he that loveth me shall be loved of my father, and I will love him and will manifest myself to him" John 14:21

The Lord Jesus said it emphatically here that one way to experience His manifest presence is by loving Him. This love entails accessing His commandments and instructions and then keeping them.

So, loving the Lord means obeying His commandments. You cannot claim to love the Lord and walk in disobedience to His instruction. *"if ye love me, keep my commandments " John 14:15*

It is in walking in obedience before the Lord that we prove our love for Him. He has given His commandments and the summary of the commandment is Love. *"A new commandment I give unto you, that ye love one another as I have loved you, that ye also love one another"* John 13:34

Every time we walk in disobedience to the Lord's instruction we are reacting against Him. Disobedience, rebellion, witchcraft, stubbornness, iniquity, and idolatry are treated as the same in the sight of the Lord and they will always make a man to miss the glory of His presence.

"For rebellion is as the sin of witchcraft and stubbornness is as iniquity and idolatry. Because thou has rejected the word of the Lord, he hath also rejected thee from being King." 1 Samuel 15:23.

ABSOLUTE FAITH AND TRUST IN GOD

"Jesus saith unto her said I not unto thee that if thou wouldest believe thou shouldest see the glory of God"? John 11:40

Faith makes us pleasing to God and attracts us to Him.

But without faith it is impossible to please him : for he that cometh to God must believe that he is, and that he is a rewarder of them that diligently seek him. Hebrews 11:6

When we live by faith in Him we are responding to Him thereby giving Him the platform to manifest His power and reveal His glory to us and in us.

When we dwell in doubt and unbelief however, we are reacting to Him and we are robbed of His power and glory.

The three Hebrew boys displayed their faith in God before Nebuchadnezzar. He revealed Himself to them in the midst of the fiery furnace.

For God to manifest Himself to us and show us His glory we must first believe Him and put our trust in Him.

Chapter Twelve

ACCESSING THE GLORY

"And the Lord saith unto Moses, I will do this thing also thou hast spoken; for thou hast found grace in my sight and I know thee by name" Exodus 33:7

The primary access to the glory of God is the grace of God. Until a man has found the grace of God he cannot access the glory of God. The glory of God becomes a mystery forever for the man who has not found the saving grace of God.

When the grace of God that brings salvation has appeared to a man then he can access the glory of God. Grace is the forerunner of the glory of God.

"For the LORD God is a sun and a shield; the LORD will give grace and glory; no good thing will he withhold from them that walk up rightly" Psalm 84:11.

The Psalmist said here that the first thing that the LORD will give before glory is grace. It is when you have found his grace and your sins have been forgiven that you are qualified to access His glory. Sin is the greatest enemy of God's glory. The eye of a sinful man cannot see the glory of God. *Roman 3:23* says it was sin that made all men fall short of the glory of God.

So, sin disqualified man from glory but grace in Christ Jesus restores our access to the glory of God. Grace came through Christ. Everything Jesus did to restore us back to God is the work of grace. *"For the law came through Moses but grace and truth came by Jesus Christ"*. **John 1:17**

So, grace is all that God has made available to us through the sacrifice of His son Jesus.

G   -   God's
R   -   Riches
A   -   At
C   -   Christ
E   -   Expense

On our own terms we are not qualified for anything but grace qualifies us. *"For by grace are ye saved through faith; and that not of yourselves; it is the gift of God; Not of works, lest any man should boast"* Eph. 2:8-9.

God told Moses, the only reason I am going to do what you have asked for and show you my glory is because you have found grace in my sight. Exodus 33:17

Grace is our surest access to the glory of God. Glory be to God for the grace that is available to us in Christ Jesus. When we receive it and maximize it then we are set for glory.

The Psalmist went further to say that after the Lord has given grace and glory He will make every good thing of life available. Remember; that glory is the manifestation of God in all His goodness to a man. *Exodus 33:19.* So, the place of His glory is the place of every good thing of life. When you access His glory you have access to all of His goodness.

However, it begins with grace you must receive grace first. Your sins must be forgiven first before you can have access to His glory that guarantees every good things of life.

That grace is available today. All you have to do is to believe in the Lord Jesus, confess your sins to Him and repent from them all. Then ask Him to save your soul and be the Lord of your life from now on. Promise Him that you will serve Him for the rest of your life as He makes His grace available to you.

If you do this with the whole of your heart then His grace will flow to you and your sins will be forgiven. You will then have access to the glory of God.

BE HUNGRY FOR HIS GLORY

Now that you have access by grace, you must show to God that you want to experience His glory by your hunger and thirst. You must have a desire for Him above everything else then you will be able to experience His glory.

You must be hungry and thirsty enough for the glory of His presence like the Psalmist if you want to experience it._*"O God, thou art my God early will I seek thee; my soul thirsteth for thee, my flesh longeth for thee in a dry and thirsty land, where no water is; To see thy power and glory"* Psalm 63:1-2.

Seek Him early; be hungry and thirsty for His presence. Let nothing else satisfy you until you experience His glory then He will reveal His glory to you.

You must be desperate in prayer like Moses and be ready to pay the price of waiting on Him until you experience His glory.

"And He said I beseech thee, show me thy glory" Exodus 33:18.

Moses would not take no for an answer. He prayed until God answered. More importantly He paid the price of staying with God before He could carry His glory. *Exodus 34:28-29.*

God's glory is still available today. Are you hungry enough? Are you willing to pay the price? Can you make the required sacrifice of staying with Him until the glory rest on you?

Printed in the United States
By Bookmasters